Henry Chester Parsons

The Reaper

And Other Poems

Henry Chester Parsons

The Reaper
And Other Poems

ISBN/EAN: 9783744709781

Printed in Europe, USA, Canada, Australia, Japan

Cover: Foto ©Thomas Meinert / pixelio.de

More available books at **www.hansebooks.com**

THE TRIAL OF THE FIRST REAPER.

"Another trial, and again
Returning from the Rockbridge plain."

THE REAPER,

AND OTHER POEMS

H. C. PARSONS

NEW-YORK

1884

To

*T*HE gentle wife
  In whom my life
    Is joyous and content;
Whose hand hath healed,
Whose faith hath sealed
The vow and sacrament.

TO MY FRIENDS.

I SAY nothing to the public, for this little book will not be offered for sale; but to you I would explain,—these poems were written because the writing rested me. They go to the printer because my child requests it. Let no one think that I am self-deceived or deluded into new paths from the daily work that satisfies my need and my ambition.

Perhaps, in the warmth of your firesides, these pages may glow with a light that is half their own, and the circle draw closer and the hour pass pleasantly; perhaps one who reads alone may find something here written that will turn his thoughts tenderly to the Virginia Mountains, or give him a clearer faith or a braver heart. Then I shall be glad.

H. C. P.

CONTENTS.

THE REAPER .   . 13

THE DIVIDED HOUSE.   19

THE BROWN, BLUE, AND GRAY .   . 23

THE SEVENTH BIRTHDAY .   27

HOW GRETCHEN OUTRODE THE FLOOD   . . 28

VIRGINIA   38

THE PRAYER FOR FROST   45

BATTLE OF LIFE .   49

HOW KATIE OUTRODE THE SUN .   . 53

THE BLUE OF THE SORROWFUL EYES   .   55

THE PRISONER RELEASED   . 57

"THE HINDOO'S SEARCH FOR TRUTH" .   58

DECEMBER 23, 1873   . 61

ILLUSTRATIONS.

THE REAPER.

THE TRIAL OF THE FIRST REAPER .   Frontispiece

THE HEART OF THE SIERRAS .   .   . 17

THE DIVIDED HOUSE.

" I 'VE SWUNG UPON THAT BROKEN GATE,

I 'VE RACED THAT TANGLED PATH "   .   21

THE BROWN, BLUE, AND GRAY.

THE BROWN, BLUE, AND GRAY   . 25

HOW GRETCHEN OUTRODE THE FLOOD.

" WHERE TREES LAY IN HER COURSE "   .   .   .   29

" WHERE FROM ROCKBRIDGE, BATH, AND HIGHLAND

MANY SWOLLEN RIVERS MEET "   . 34

VIRGINIA.

" FULL WERE THY HILLS, AND FRUITFUL WAS THE LAND " .   39

" TILL THY HISTORIC JAMES " 43

THE PRAYER FOR FROST.

" STORM AND SNOW AND HAIL

FROM THE NORTH " .   47

BATTLE OF LIFE.

" FROM HILLS WHERE PLUMÉD TORRENTS RISE " .   . 51

THE REAPER.

"Another trial, and again
Returning from the Rockbridge plain."

I.

⊃K to the endless labor the sickle-bearers turned;
.nd all the eyes that lifted, and all the hearts that yearned!
to the even contest, the hard and narrow way,
 every day repeateth the need of yesterday.

 shall not rest till even, they shall not buy or build;
ield is never finished, the garner never filled;
ıarvest skies are brazen, the fierceness of the sun
ıpered falls on fainting men since first the world begun.

ıck to shadow Indus, no palm in Palestine,
ırvest-home with laughter, no dance upon the green;
eapers and the gleaners, through all the ages told,
waited in the market-place, where men are bought and sold.

The world in vain hath sought it, and now the world is old,
The altars smoked for ages, and yet no prophet told:
But turn not back, McCormick! the time is drawing nigh,
Thy hand is on the secret spring where silent forces lie.

The time is past for wailing, the time is come for song;
The tale—across the ocean and all the hills along,
Through vales of Andalusia and valleys of Cashmere,
And 'on the Montenegrin fields, where stars are shining near;

Along the shores of Chili, girt with the awful snow,
Across the lifted prairie where Don and Dnieper flow—
Will bear the joyful tidings: The giant reaper moves,
For Life hath touched the points of steel and runs the iron grooves.

II.

In London's Crystal Palace, the stateliest ever seen,
To thee the Council medal is given by the Queen;
To far and fair Vienna, to Lisle and Hamburg called,
Thy tribute comes, through royal hands, from millions dis-
    enthralled;

Paris proclaims the contest, while all her bells are rung,
With all the world in waiting, and all her banners hung:
They come from every nation, and over every sea,
And when the honors all are told, the highest is for thee.

Rejoice, ye burdened peoples! and shout, ye nations, when
One cometh to the rescue with thrice a million men:
Crown! Crown the feast with plenty, bring cymbal, lute, and lyre,
And bid the souls of peasants drink of daring and desire!

Refulgent Sun, flood India and yellow-fringed Algiers!
Gild broadened blades of Holland and Sweden's silver spears!
And down the far Pacific slope let all thy wealth be rolled,
Until the purple seas shall stay the broken sea of gold.

Let all thy fires be kindled, and all thy darts be hurled,
A line that never wavers shall follow round the world;
Will capture all thy treasure, and every field that waves:
The host obeys a royal will, but *men* are not the slaves.

III.

Where went the host from harvest? Some laced the land with steel;
Beneath their mighty cargoes, the banded derricks reel;
Their fires are on the mountain, their lights are in the foam,
And some have sought the Golden Fleece, and now they bring it
        home.

Some drove the Sutro tunnel; some trace the silver lead;
Some in the Iron City, insatiate forges feed;
Some have struck the rock of oil, and some are in the mills,
And some are building palaces upon a thousand hills.

A rod hath touched the glacier and led it through the plain,
A hand hath held the ocean and bound it with a chain;
The heart of the Sierras receives the fatal stroke,
The Mississippi passeth slow beneath the iron yoke.

A shaft hath pierced the mountain and wrenched its portal wide,
And rocked in restful slumber the distant pilgrims ride;
The storm hath told its secret, the midnight tale is known,
A whisper breathed in Oregon is whispered now in Rome.

The mirage ends in miracles, and Egypt, on her knees,
Sees ships that sail the desert like ships that sail the seas;
The Esquimau is hiding, Arabia lifts her veil,
As through the sundered continents the prows of Europe sail.

Well hast thou won, McCormick, the tribute that we bring;
Of all the lords of labor, we name thee as the king:
Strong arms that never shorten, and heart that never grieves,
And all the autumn winds to bear the rustle of thy sheaves!

[My attention was called to the work the reaper was doing by the remarks of two great men, made about twenty-five years ago. William H. Seward said that, "owing to Mr. McCormick's invention, the line of civilization moved westward thirty miles each year." Reverdy Johnson stated that "the invention was an annual source of revenue to the United States of more than fifty millions of dollars." It is hard to overestimate the forces that this discovery has set free and the opportunity that it has given for thought and new invention; there are half a million machines now in use, each doing the work of from six to ten men.

The recognition that has been given furnishes a long list of medals and honors, from among which I mention the following: Grand Council Medal, London, 1851; Grand Gold Medal, Paris, 1855; Grand Gold Medal, Hamburg, 1863; Grand Prize, Paris, 1867; Cross of the Legion of Honor, 1867; two Grand Gold Medals, Vienna, 1873; two Medals, U. S. Centennial, 1876; Gold Medal, Royal Agricultural Society, England, 1878 and 1881; Grand Prize, Paris, 1878; Officer of the Legion of Honor, 1878; Grand Gold Medal, Melbourne, 1880; Gold Medal, New Zealand Exposition, 1882; Grand Gold Medal, Rome, 1883.]

THE HEART OF THE SIERRAS.

THE DIVIDED
HOUSE.

NO firelight gilds the vines
    that creep
Across the narrow sash,
No bucket hangs from bending
    sweep,
No˙swing from leaning ash.

No birds are nesting in the trees,
    No fowl are in the yard;
The russet hives have lost their
    bees,
    The riven door is barred.

The gladdest hours I ever knew
    Were in that silent hall;
The sweetest fruit that ever grew
    Hung on that garden-wall.

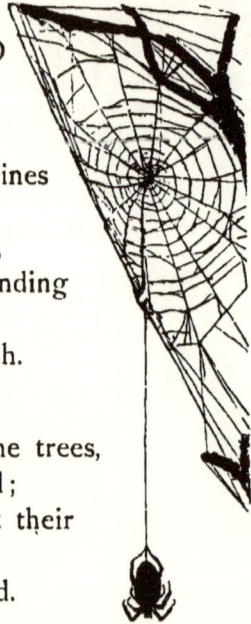

Of all the glorious trees, not one
 Escaped the bolt or blight,
And here, beneath a cloudless sun,
 Lie shades of endless night.

I 've seen a lawn like velvet there,
 And roses white as snow ;
I 've seen an angel on that stair,
 I 've looked on Heaven, below.

I 've swung upon that broken gate,
 I 've raced that tangled path,
And never dreamed that sire could hate,
 Or brothers part in wrath.

THE DIVIDED HOUSE.

"I 've swung upon that broken gate,
I 've raced that tangled path."

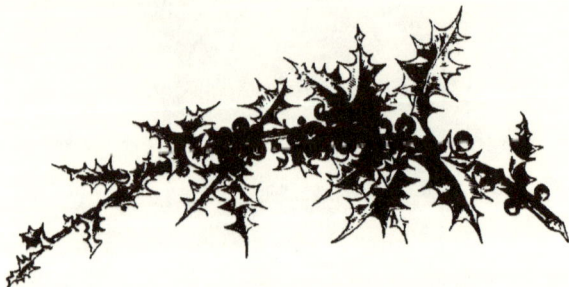

THE BROWN, BLUE, AND GRAY.

THE watchers were weary, and train-time was nigh;
   There was protest and pleading and tearful good-bye;
We laid the three gently upon the white bed,
And tenderly pillowed each sorrowful head.
The lips were all silent, and soft were the sighs;
The lashes were hiding the beautiful eyes:
On the right lay the dark waves that rippled in gold,
On the left flowed the silver that never was told,
   And the wing of the raven was there.

The brown eyes said, closing, "I hope you 'll be late";
The blue eyes yet trembled—"How long can you wait?"
The gray, dark with pleading, were closing in prayer;
The hush of God's angel was stilling the air.

The brown hands were crossed and pressed in their place;
The white hand lay lost in the fold of the lace;
In velvet and dimples, the hand that was stirred;
The breath of the sleepers was all that I heard,
    And the shriek of the incoming train.

I twice kissed the proud lips,—the ruby lips twice;
The lips that were pouting, I turned to them thrice,
Then hurried forth blind in the pitiless rain
And into the night on the outgoing train.
But I think, while I bent over tresses and bands,
All my heart-strings were caught by the motionless hands;
For wherever I wait, and wherever I roam,
They are driving me on, they are drawing me home,
    While I dream of the brown, blue, and gray.

THE BROWN, BLUE, AND GRAY.

THE SEVENTH BIRTHDAY.

SHE knew the morning would be fair,
  And every bird would sing;
She came as lightly on the stair,
  As lark upon the wing.

My lady's cheek was all aglow,
  Her blue eyes were alight,
They linked the silver curb-chain low,
  And drew the red girth tight.

She gayly bent to giddy flight,
  Her silver tresses shone,
The horse she rode was black as night—
  It came a panting roan.

HOW GRETCHEN OUTRODE THE FLOOD.

THROUGHOUT the night from glen to glen, from cliff to
    cliff, the call
That summoned every crested stream to break the mountain wall!
A march was in the cañon's beat and in the valley's throb;
The signals flew from Otter's Peaks and flashed from Elliot's Knob;
The ribboned lances of the plain were stacked in golden ranks,
The dikes were down, the guards were gone, the river leapt the
    banks.

I.

Bright flood of noontide swept the sky and turned the tempest's
    force
As Gretchen tried the mountain path, where trees lay in her
    course.
The gray horse leapt the rushing streams and flew the riven oak;
He madly dared the breaking bridge, and cleared it as it broke.
When by her mother's ruined home she drew the flowing rein,
No scythe was in the aftermath, no sickle on the grain —
But down the lines of circling foam, the reapers' level path,
And tossed against the russet hills, the harvesting of wrath.

"WHERE TREES LAY IN HER COURSE."

She turned as to a battle-field—she bent her queenly form,
And felt across the trembling air the pulses of the storm;
She leaned unmindful of the woe, with blue eyes wonder-wide,
Her loosened tresses falling to the horse's silver side.
Through broken branches swinging wide, wrenched in the night
    assail,
The sun fell on her golden hair and on his coat of mail.

With halting words old Friday told, as one who tells a dream,
How Judith with her cabin had been carried down the stream;
And how she saw and cried to her, abandoned to her fate:—
Though on the wind her mistress rode, alas! she rode too late.

II.

Slowly turned the startled maiden to the creatures crouching there,
And they shrunk before her anger who were dumb in their despair.
"Could you fear when I was coming?   Are the strong men
    never brave?
She was old, and sick, and crippled, yet no hand was quick to
    save.
Draw the girth and break the curb-chain!   Oh, my horse of
    noble blood,
There is fearful work before us; Roland, we must cheat the
    flood!"

Judith's weary eyes were closing when they caught the sudden
    gleam
Of a white cloud on the hill-side, and she fancied in her dream,
That again her Gretchen, riding, won the races at the farm,
And from habit waved her kerchief, held it with her rigid arm;

Closed her weary eyes and patient, lest the vision should be gone,
Shutting out the skies and angels, shutting in a dream of home.

Gretchen held the bridle firmly in the long and doubtful race,
Miles on miles the gray horse galloped with his great and
    tireless pace,
Dashing through the dark backwater, flying past the gleam-
    ing dike,
While afar the iron hoof-beat told the measures of the pike,
Till the call of crimson kerchief, and the stroke upon his mane,
Brought the stride of old Abdallah, as he crossed the flying plain.

By the ferry of Glen-Allen, in the shelter of the shore,
Tommy Coleman with the drift-hook and Hugh Xavier at the
    oar.

(At the tournament in April, with the burdened lance at rest,
Many rode beneath the arches, but the tallest knight rode best;
And where all the birds were singing and where all the fields
    were green,
With the boast so long translated, crowned the gentle Gretchen
    queen.*)

"She that sinks is my dear servant. Xavier, prove thy knight-
    hood now ;
Well I see the fearful peril, but my hand will point thy prow."
"Laggard comes the fettered forest! she is just before the pine,
Winds are holding back the driftwood ; bend the oar and throw
    the line ! "

* Do not scorn or lightly weigh
Strength disclosed in mimic fray,
For it waits till shown by thee
Highest test of chivalry.

32

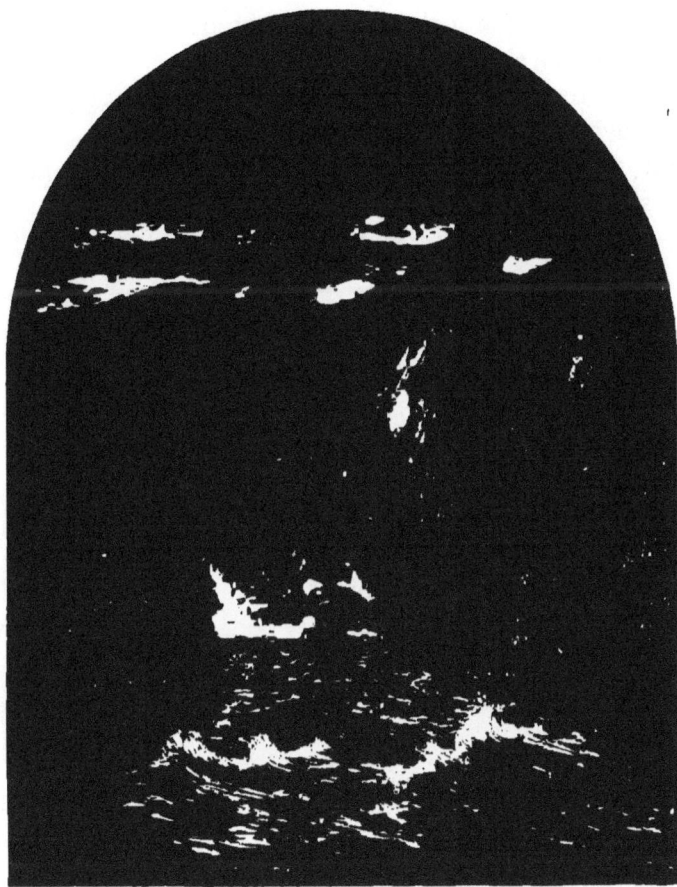

"WHERE FROM ROCKBRIDGE, BATH, AND HIGHLAND MANY SWOLLEN
RIVERS MEET."

Judith passed, while pale men answered: "Human arm can
    never save,
Where the trees and houses crashing are the playthings of the
    wave!"
Sadly from the river turned she — turned to cliff and mountain
    side —
Tried again the bristling fences, and again outran the tide.

III.

Where the great defiant mountains crouch between the iron feet,
Where from Rockbridge, Bath, and Highland many swollen
    rivers meet,
Where a dark and troubled ocean sweeps Virginia's fairest plain,
And no path is on the mountain and no boat is on the main.
"Roland, we can go no farther, and I hear the swelling sound
Of the falls where, swiftly hurried, my poor Judith will be drowned.

Slaves and strong-armed men are waiting while the tides defiant
    roll,
Only thy strength now remaineth, and the courage of my soul.
Good horse, save me, swim the river; do not fail me in my need;
Trust again my skill and courage—I can trust my matchless
    steed."
Roland turned his great eyes pleading, driven to the river's edge,
Drew his cringeing feet together, slid across the fatal ledge.

On the heights no cannon thundered, cross nor banner led the way,
Human voice nor eye encouraged where the path of peril lay:
In the eddy, on the surges, on the river dark and swift,
To the rescue of the dying, down the dark line of the drift.

Horse and graceful rider turning, while the woman from the storm
Wondered much how God's own angel came to her in Gretchen's
    form.

But at last the double burden and the horse's fearful cry
Told the noble-hearted maiden that the end was drawing nigh :
"Roland, save us, me and Judith; save yourself, my noble horse!"
Rang the clear voice of the rider, but it called no equal force.
Nothing now can stem the current, and the hungry vortex calls:
Only one chance now remaineth—"Roland, turn and shoot the
    falls!"

IV.

On the windrow of the torrent, where the way is thin and high,
Where the lines of swift outriders gleam like coursers of the sky,
Through the trough of curling breakers, on the bank of level foam,
Buoyant on the lifting billow, resting on the rising dome.
For a moment, then forever in the hand of God who wills,
On the white crest of the rapids, through the black gate of the hills,
Cliff and cavern leaned and thundered, cloud and pillar closed
    the way,
Night was on the trackless river 'neath the arches of the spray.
Madly came the flood's battalions, breaking lances on the walls,
Level leapt the driven river from the breaker of the falls.

Flood of sunlight through the valley, flash of crystals far and nigh,
Molten crags upon the mountain, molten mountains in the sky,
Beaten lawn, where winds had woven in the green with brown
    and gold,
All the autumn torches lighted, all the trailing banners told,
As along the lifted forest and across the purple sea,
From the bright and level lances all the wounded shadows flee,

Wide the silver cloud was parted and the burnished gates were
wide,
When the rider came in triumph, with the rescued at her side,
And the storm king's brightest jewels crowned the victor in
the list
'Gainst the tempest's whitest horses through the portals of the
mist.
Only with a final effort Roland reeled across the loam,
Though his feet were on the meadow, while his breast was in
the foam.
Heeding not the shouts and glory, and the people gathered there,
Gretchen kneeled beside the woman in the attitude of prayer.

VIRGINIA.

A WAKE! Virginia, awake!
  'T is time to break the double century spell;
The hammer now upon the matin bell
Beats final fateful stroke; it is not well
To sleep, till trembling iron strikes the knell
      Of those who cannot wake.

      Arise and look around!
Thy dream was fair, but castles do not stand,—
The level waste extends on every hand.
Full were thy hills, and fruitful was the land,
Strong were thy sons, and every wind was bland,—
      And yet are ashes here.

      The tournament is done.
Thy level lance is broken, and the serious care
That made so tame thy sisters, brought them treasures rare,
And walls their harvest-home with fruits more fair
Than flowers; and shining heights thou didst not dare
      Are banner-swept by them.

"FULL WERE THY HILLS, AND FRUITFUL WAS THE LAND."

We will not blame the past,
Or count its sad illusions; it was very great
To found and wisely rule earth's proudest State;
And when it pleased thee, careless of thy fate,
To smite its pillars till the world did wait
　　　To see the great towers fall.

There yet is time to learn,
And subject to command. The swift power that fills
Thy river-banks shall work for him who wills;
And black slaves prisoned in thy lifted hills
Await thy order, while a strong life thrills
　　　The veins of all thy sons.

Thy treasures are not told.
Stores of coal and iron, gold and salt and oil,
Fill shoreless caverns, and thy fountains boil
With living waters, and thy unspent soil
Awaits a longer plowshare; for their mighty toil
　　　Thy subjects are impatient.

But know, thy sons must lead
And bravely work! No white hand ever broke
The padlock of the hills; no gentle stroke
Wakes mountain-echoes where, in fire and smoke,
The black-starred crown is wrought, and forged the iron yoke
　　　For tribute-paying peoples.

Await no stranger aid!
Arise! command and strike! Unlock thy store!
Unchain thy ebon slaves and bid them smite the ore
That veins thy mountains, till red rivers pour
Into the plain, and burdened wharves shall brace the shore
      Of the inreaching ocean!

      Till thy historic James
Shall cease its sport and, vexed and chained and slow,
Shall learn its daily toil; till its broad face shall glow
With blazing furnaces; till the whole world shall know
A lane of cities to the ships that daily go
      To many distant ports!

      O bid thy minions light the fires
Upon a million hearths; and bid them place thy honest seal
Upon earth's whitest flour; and stamp the brightest steel
That wins earth's battles; and the farthest iron keel
That parts the seas; O bid them drive the mightiest wheel
      In all the workshops of the world!

"TILL THY HISTORIC JAMES."

THE PRAYER FOR FROST.

MARY, my only child,
    You woke me when you cried.
    Or else I should have died;
    Throw all the windows wide
        To the North!

Still the soft breezes play
    And fill the haunted room
    With flood of sweet perfume,
    Of perfect flower and bloom
        From the South.

My child, you were too young
    To know the fearful years
    So full of hates and tears;
    To see the burdened biers
        Of the South.

But now the times are changed,—
    And for an hundred days
    The Northern people prays,
    And blessings load the ways
        From the North.

And yet, and yet we die!
    I lived, I know not how!
    Six times upon the brow
    I sealed my dead, and now—
        Your lips must

The night is dark and still;
    I hear the muffled feet
    That hourly pass the street;
    They will return, and meet—
        At this door.

I feel a cooler breath;
    Perhaps I yet may stay
    And see another day;—
    Ah me! that I should pray
        Against my flowers.

Yet, let the North wind rage,
    Smite with the hand of mail,
    Strike with the iron flail,
    Bring storm and snow and hail
        From the North!

Spare not the beauteous land—
    Bring healing in death's wing,
    O that my knell could ring
    The coming Northern king
        To save the South.

"STORM AND SNOW AND HAIL
FROM THE NORTH."

BATTLE OF LIFE.

THE widest war in all the world
   Is where no banners are unfurled,—
No shining lance is held. or hurled:
   Battle of Life.
Deep in the ages was begun,
And is renewed with every sun,
While fields and forts are daily won
   In endless strife.

The great war hath its dungeons deep,
Its tentless fields where gleaners sleep,
Its dark defiles where white wolves leap,
   Its nameless dead.
But still the armies face the west,
And every morrow is the best,
And every night brings earlier rest
   And whiter bread.

This war, too, hath its heroes grand,
And at their wise and high command
The furies of the sea and land
    Are allies kind.
From hills where pluméd torrents rise,
From caves where primal forest lies,
The help that leapeth from the skies
    And rides the wind.

Fair cities rise where forests fall,
The spoils are many, and for all,
From beaten lawn to bannered wall,
    The conqueror creates.
Before his fires the day is dim,
His coursers pass the purple rim,
The smoking gorge is bridged for him,
    And swung the granite gate.

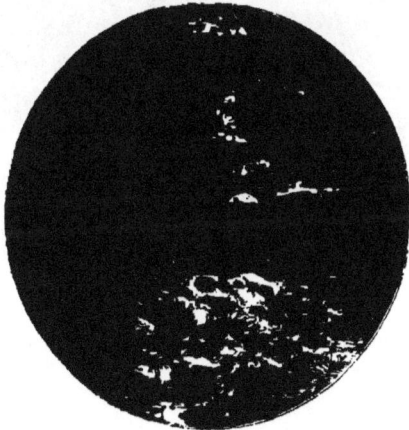

"FROM HILLS WHERE PLUMÉD TORRENTS RISE."

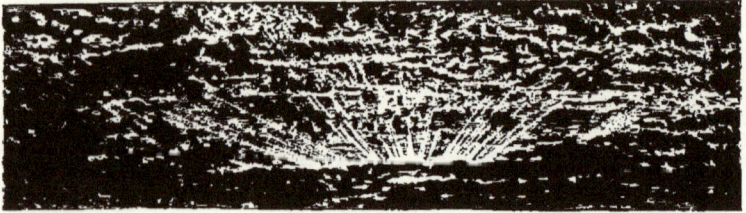

HOW KATIE OUTRODE THE SUN.

I DREAMT of a vale in the storm-haunted hills,
  Where the fields were but folds and the rivers were rills;
Where the white clouds like horses ran yoked to their shadows,
And the rain fell in mists on the blue-broidered meadows.

I dreamt of a child with brown gold-threaded hair,
In the gray of the dawn on the stile's silver stair;
White plume and blue habit, impatiently standing,
While the night-waves broke soft on the moss-matted landing.

I dreamt of a mare that came black as the night,
Save the star on her front and the hoof on the right;
The child calling pet names, the mare gently neighing,
For the sign in the East, a moment delaying.

The hoof-beat is loud on the Hurricane bridge,
They have passed the great oak on St. Anthony's Ridge,
They are lost in the mists of the Whispering Valley,
Where the white deer was shot at the Silverhorn rally.

Where no one may follow and none can recall,
They are leaping the chasm and scaling the wall;
Up the bright slope are turning, yet higher and higher,
Where the ledges are gold and the pines are on fire.

I dreamt that my child had outridden the sun;
At the gate of the day the bright banner was won,
And never had victor such regal adorning
As the mantle that fell from the lap of the morning.

THE BLUE OF THE SORROWFUL EYES.

THE sentinel peaks tore the hurrying clouds,
    And threw the white shreds at their feet;
The voice of the pines was the shriek of the shrouds
    Where breakers off Hatteras meet.
But in mirrors and mists, and openings fair,
    And banners that fall from the skies,
The mother sees only the brown, tangled hair,
    And the blue of the sorrowful eyes.

Where Battlement Rocks are a thousand feet high
    And New River is foam at their base,
When wind-shaken spears are piercing the sky
    And echoes are filling the place,
Through shock and alarm, and legion and lair,
    In the twilight that everywhere lies,
Away from the light of the summer-kissed hair,
    And the blue of the sorrowful eyes.

Where red-bannered towers lean far overhead
   And escarpments have melted like snow,
Where the spray of the cataract's folly is spread
   On the smoke of the battle below,
The train like a shuttle is shot through the air,
   Through portal and tunnel it flies,
But her heart bears her back to the wind-loosened hair,
   And the blue of the sorrowful eyes.

Where river-fiends toss the black boulders like sand
   And night-winds eternally moan,
They sweep through the arches and passages grand
   And places that never were known;
Blue Gauley waits shy at the shimmering stair,
   Kanawha hath sunny surprise,
But the mother sees only the braided brown hair
   And the blue of the sorrowful eyes.

THE PRISONER RELEASED.

I COULD stand and look at the stars all night,
  Where tides run with wreaths to the rivers and rills;
  Where the sea-breezes play with the wind from the hills;
  Where by land or by sea man shall go where he wills;
I am free man again, and free man of right.

I could stand and look at the stars all night;
  For months that were years they have prisoned my stars;
  My silver-veiled Venus and red-hooded Mars
  Were fretted and framed by the merciless bars
That shaded their glory or shivered their light.

I will stand and look at the stars all night;
  I will wait in the shadow and lee of the tower,
  Till morning shall come with his magical power;
  Perhaps in the flame of that wonderful hour
The prison will tremble and pass from my sight.

"THE HINDOO'S SEARCH FOR TRUTH."

AN ANSWER.

" All the world over, I wander in lands I never have trod,
Are the people eternally seeking the signs and steps of a God."

YES, all the pleading nations weep beneath the silent skies,
And all the echoes of the hills repeat despairing cries ;
A million altars light their fires, and night is on the land,
A million priests repeat a tale that none can understand.

Hill, plain, and shore are sounding far, and seas incessant roar,
Yet they were voiceless from the first, and are for evermore ;
And death is always touching eyes yet mad with great desire ;
Above us roll the loosened winds, beneath a sea of fire.

The mirrors are all breaking now, the standards are not true,
The web of all our weary work will vanish with the dew ;
The lamp-lit camp on evening sands is on the morrow gone,
The winds that bear our ashes hence will smite the shrines of stone.

The songs of Bethlehem flood the nave till iron arches bend,
And India's penitential cry the walls of sapphire rend ;
But still the maddening echoes fall, the answers never come,
The oracles forever dark, the gods forever dumb.

And yet, because beneath the hills ye found the steps of God,
His lesson in the flaming sky and on the flowering sod,
With cubits ye have madly tried to measure endless span,
And made a God, on marble, write eternal guide for man.

Ye would not hear the inward voice or shut your eyes and see,
But, searching for the Holy Ghost, ye crossed the frozen sea;
And far beyond the desert sands, and far beyond the snow,
Ye wandered and despairing cried, "What do the wisest know?"

In Indian woods are mystic sounds and fires in northern skies,
And pious hands support and lead and martyrs lift their cries;
But lost in trackless forests deep or driven upon seas,
Their bearings are the sounding rocks, their guidons are the trees.

But ye have faith, and know it not, and doubting ye believe,
And while ye search and cry in vain, the spirit ye receive!
We rest upon the beetling cliff, and know it will not fall,
We sleep where threatening rivers rise, and hear the ocean call.

Though bleeding feet are driven hard and never reach the goal,
The fire hath never tempered yet the steel to pierce the soul;
In vain the furious fever burns, the lightning strikes in vain,
The fire may in the stubble rage, the garner hath the grain.

The countless swift processions pass and press into the night,
With banners falling on the left, and falling on the right;
And yet a sign is over them, if they would lift their eyes,
And yet a voice is reaching them, if they would still their cries.

A sign that standeth fair and high, yet without flame or form,
A voice that cometh sure and nigh in sorrow and in storm,
A voice that hath no language, yet calleth every name,
A voice that little children hear and women wrapped in flame.

Silent may stand the answered priest, and letterless the scroll,
And lens and nerves may never bring the light that fills the soul;
But yet, before the evening's gate, beyond the day's annoy,
Thy patient soul shall find the light and wonder in its joy.

And thou shalt hear the voices shout that fell in stifled cries,
And thou shalt see the risen faith beyond the riven skies,
And thou shalt see the banners wave, the banners that were furled,
And learn the recompense that waits the labor of the world.

Where the translucent mountains rise, where living waters flow,
The mountains crowned with whiter wreaths than Himalaya's snow,
Where all the rivers are alight and all the sands are gold,
The groves of God eternal stand, and there the truth is told.

DECEMBER 23, 1873.

*S*HE *may not tell the rubric well,*
    Or well intone the psalm:
  But to her soul the thunder roll
Is stiller than the calm.

Night closing wild, a moaning child,
    A hunter without game;
Uncertain glow of embers low,
    A sudden burst of flame.

The blinded quail struck window-rail,
    And fell beside her chair;
The mother felt, before she knelt,
    That God had answered prayer.

www.ingramcontent.com/pod-product-compliance
Lightning Source LLC
Chambersburg PA
CBHW021640270326
41931CB00008B/1093